99

OLD WHITE MEN JOKES

Compiled and edited

By Wycliffe Horse

Copyright © 2018 Wycliffe Horse
All rights reserved.
ISBN-13: 978-1508903758
ISBN-10: 1508903751

DEDICATION

I dedicate this book to my high school art teacher, Miss Flossie Schmidt. God, I sure am glad we never got caught. Flossie, you would be an old woman now, except you died. I will always remember afternoon study hall with you in that janitor's closet. Now every time I smell a wet mop I get sort of excited in a peculiar way.

ACKNOWLEDGMENTS

I do not know the origin of most of these jokes; I only know that most of them are very old. I remember kicking the slats out of my cradle the first time I heard some of them because they were so incredibly funny.

YOU CAN'T TELL JOKES ABOUT THEM ANY MORE!

You can't have fun anymore. Used to be you could pick any group of people other than your own and tell crude cruel jokes about them. Now that behaviour is not proper. All those groups, you know who they are, are off limits – except, wait, there is one group left: old white men.

So put on your metaphorical seat belt and get ready to hear some of those old jokes with a new twist. Just for fun, try to guess the group that was originally the butt of the joke before it was converted, here, to an acceptable Old White Men form. You will never guess.

Silly Old White Man, Specimen 1

"The Enforcer"

BABY SKUNKS

Pierpont and Cornelius, two old white men, were duck hunting in Southwest Louisiana in the United States of America As they drove their sports utility vehicle, a British Land Rover, along a back road they hit a bump.

"My good and lifelong friend," Cornelius said to Pierpont who was driving, "I do believe that you have run over a small mammal native to this North American terrain!"

"Goodness," Pierpont said as he proceeded to maneuverer the sports utility vehicle to the side of the road. "Let us pray that that is not the case for we are conservatives in the true sense of the word, that is to say we actually conserve things!"

Upon exiting the vehicle Cornelius said, "My friend Pierpont, the small mammal dead here before us that you have run over is a North American skunk."

"That is very bad," Pierpont said with remorse.

"Yes," said Cornelius, "but this situation is far worse than that for you see before you three baby skunks, no doubt the progeny of the mother skunk!"

"My goodness," said Pierpont, falling into a deeper depression. "Now these small innocent creatures are orphaned because of me! I must make this right!"

"What will you do?"

"I shall take the three small baby mammals home with me and raise them myself. Indeed, they will sleep in the bed that belongs to me and my wife Victori Indeed, they shall sleep between me and Victoria."

"But, my friend Pierpont, what about the smell?"

"Well," declared Pierpont, "those baby skunks will just have to get used to the smell, same as I did."

Silly Old White Man, Specimen 2

"The Diplomat"

[9]

SNAKE BITE

Pierpont and Cornelius were in the woods hunting squirrels when Cornelius paused to urinate. Out of a shrub pops a rattlesnake which bites him on the very tip of his penis.

"Ouch," said Cornelius. "That hurt!" But giving the matter further consideration he called for his friend, Pierpont. "Come here, my friend Pierpont! Something has happened here that may put my life in danger!"

"Yes, I see" said Pierpont. "It appears that a snake has bitten you on your male appendage."

"Yes, indeed that appears to be the case," replied Cornelius. "And it seems wise at this point to seek the assistance of medical professionals, of which there are none in this wooded setting."

"And how do you propose that we do that?" responded Pierpont.

"Although my consciousness is rapidly fading due to the venom injected into my circulatory system by the viper, and since you do not possess the knowledge needed to save me, I suggest that you trot your ass over to the nearby village and locate medical professionals that are normally found in adequate supply in such population centers of our civilization."

"OK," said Pierpont, as he trotted his ass away with a destination of the nearby village.

Arriving at the nearby village Pierpont located an abundance of medical professionals. Unfortunately all of these medical professionals were busy with a recently occurring train wreck that had created unspeakable carnage.

"We are too busy to personally attend to your friend," said one of the doctors. "But you can solve the problem yourself with a simple procedure. With your pocked knife make a small incision at the point of the snake bite. Place your lips on this incision and suck the poison out."

"Oh," replied Pierpont, who then trotted back to the location of his friend Cornelius, who, indeed was fading fast.

In his now weak voice Cornelius asked, "What did the doctor say?"

Pierpont, looking at the swollen snake-bitten penis, replied, "He said that you are going to die."

That concludes the snake bite joke, which was very funny, but one thing must be added as a lead-in to the next joke. Cornelius survived in spite of the lack of help from Pierpont. It happened that an old white man was passing and stopped to help. I cannot tell you a lot about the man because of the mandates of this document which require that I not classify people by race, religion, or national origin. Let's just say that he was an old white man who knew a lot about using knives to cut on penises, usually the penises of babies, and only on the foreskins of those baby penises. This man knew how to make the incision at the snake bite and he did not seem to mind at all as he sucked the snake's venom from Cornelius.

After completion of the venom removal process the "Good Samaritan" old white man remarked, "Well I see you are already circumcised, so I suppose my work here is done."

Because his treatment had been delayed Cornelius suffered some illness and had to go to the hospital for additional procedures, which leads us into the next joke.

CHOCOLATE PUDDING

Cornelius lay in his hospital bed, very ill, unable to take food by mouth. He was wasting away. Of course he was receiving glucose and other nutrients by an intravenous feed, a needle in his arm connected to a clear plastic bag hanging on a pole. Drip, drip, drip went the intravenous contraption, but Cornelius continued to waste away. Something additional had to be done or he would die of starvation.

You may have heard of rectal feeding, that is, providing the body with nutrients, but in the unique path of feeding it up the patient's rectum. I know it sounds bizarre; when I first heard of it I thought it must be a joke. But no, rectal feeding is used in extreme, dire circumstances. In fact it was used on prisoners at Guantanamo. The United States of America had rounded up some people from other nations and locked them up without charges for a decade or more. Seeing their plight as hopeless these men stopped eating food. So these men were on a United States Navy base at

Guantanamo Cuba, starving themselves to death. Embarrassed by the prisoner's blatant show of force, the United States decided to force feed these men. Rectal feeding was used. It was great. The shackled men could not stop the food that was pumped up their asses.

Back to Cornelius: The doctors informed him of the decision to feed him with a tube up his rectum. Cornelius agreed to the procedure.

Soon that tube was up in there. The doctors had discussed what sort of nutrient might be best. They decided on chocolate pudding, since it has lots of sugar and other things a human body could use.

The chocolate pudding was served hot to better help it be absorbed by the intestines as the gooey mixture entered the human body in the opposite direction from that which was intended by nature.

Cornelius began to scream in agony.

"What is wrong? What is wrong?" asked an attending medical person. "Is the chocolate pudding too hot?"

"No! No!" said Cornelius. "It is too sweet!"

That was the Chocolate Pudding joke and boy was it funny. And to end it on a cheerful note, Cornelius survived and was discharged from the hospital with only a few curious lingering side effects.

Cornelius was unlike his friend Pierpont who lived in a blissful state with a wife and some pet skunks. Cornelius was an old bachelor, but after his medical procedures he became easily aroused in a sexual way. Perhaps the snake bite had injected something like The Fountain of Youth into his man parts.

This leads us to the next joke.

THE KITCHEN SINK

Cornelius was looking for a wife. Though he was old and white, this would be his first wife. Yet the newly awakened yearnings of his loins must be attended to. He had heard about computer dating, bar hopping, and going to church, all as a means of getting laid. He could not hold his whiskey and going to church just to get a bed partner seemed to be just too much. He decided on computer dating. He lied about his age on his profile. He put a lot of other crap in the profile; stuff he thought would make him appealing to young women.

Based on his profile Cornelius soon had a date to meet a twenty-something woman at The Red Lobster restaurant. And there she was, Gothic, lots of tattoos, and body piercings in unusual places, some not visible to the naked eye, but which would be visible if Cornelius ever got her naked. Her name was Lolita.

"You're an old son-of-a-bitch," Lolita said on first seeing Cornelius. "I hope you got money."

I should point out that Lolita talks dirty. I will be toning down her dialogue a bit. For example, "F-Bombs" will be replaced in creative ways.

"Where's your flipping bitchin bike," Lolita asked. "I bet it's a big Harley Hog! Flipping A, I love those...."

"Well, actually," replied Cornelius, "it is a Schwinn ten-speed. I did mention that I was a biker in my profile. But I must admit I have not had it out on the road for quite some time."

"Well, flip me!" Lolita said.

"Well, of course, I was hoping for that, too. But at a later date, as I am a conservative."

"Well," she said, somewhat dismayed. "You got a ten speed bike. Got a ten-inch-cock?"

"Oddly enough, since the snake bite, it might actually be that long. I have been keeping a record of its progress, for medical reasons, of course." Cornelius removed some photos from his wallet and handed them to Lolita.

"Jesus flipping Christ!" she exclaimed, looking at the photos with great interest. "I could sure as flip choke on this; this thing is more than a mouthful."

Cornelius did not know what to make of Lolita's last statement, though there was something about it that excited him. His male junk began to expand somewhat within his pleated, cuffed trousers, a sensation he had seldom had prior to the snake bite, but to him was both pleasing and disturbing as it sometimes left a sticky, wet residue in his boxer shorts.

"Hey, I tell you what," she said. "With this pecker and a good bank account, I might just have an interest in you."

"Well," said Cornelius, removing a crumpled paper from his wallet, "here is a spreadsheet outlining my financial holdings."

She looked at the paper for quite some time. "Flip me," she said. "You're loaded, old man, both at the bank and in your flippin britches." After another moment of contemplation she added, "And if you could rent that snake out, the one that bit you on the dick to other old men like yourself, you could flippin double your assets! Old flippers like you would pay a flipping fortune to have a flippin tally whacker like yours!"

Skipping over some of the mostly amusing details, Cornelius and Lolita soon set a date to go to the courthouse and get married.

Cornelius had not had proper intercourse with a woman in many years. The times he thought he recalled he was not one-hundred percent sure that what he had been with was actually a woman, as the scene was usually dark, the hour late, and Cornelius was drunk. Lolita withheld sex until the wedding night. She said, "My mama told me that a man getting free milk ain't a gonna buy no cow. Nothing personal, old man, but I'm waiting till the papers are signed before you get into this beaver!"

The anticipation of the upcoming marital consummation began to worry Cornelius. He sought counsel from his friend Pierpont.

"Hey, don't worry about it, old chap. It will all come back to you, like riding a bicycle. Just remember this, take **the hardest thing you have in the house and put it where she pees**!" Pierpont said to Cornelius.

On the wedding night Lolita slipped into a sheer nightgown and waited spread eagle in the bedroom.

Cornelius took his complete set of golf clubs and put them in the kitchen sink. The golf club set was the **hardest thing he had in the house!**

OK, that's it, that's the joke.

But wait, there's more, and leading into the next joke, Lolita after waiting a while came to the kitchen. "What the flip are you doing?" she asked. After some convoluted dialogue Lolita grabbed Cornelius by the crotch and led into the bedroom, where they made **The- Beast- With- Two- Backs** *(coitus)*.

TOO MANY CHILDREN

It seemed no time at all before Lolita began to swell in the middle. Six months after she wed Cornelius she delivered a premature baby boy, eleven-pounds and four ounces, emerging with a shock of bright red hair.

Lolita, like Cornelius, had not fully disclosed her past on the computer dating application. She had three children by previous relationships with three different men. Lolita brought along her mother to help care for the bastards, aged three to seven, and none were at all gleeful about their new baby brother.

"At least this one has papers," Lolita's mother said. "I told her if she was a going to put out she should at least get paid, or get married!"

"Mom," Lolita objected. "Most of those men gave me money or jewellery or both."

Dismayed, Cornelius made an appointment with his doctor and long-time-friend, I. Will Kutchokokoff, M.D.

Doctor Kutchokokoff was a vain old white man who never said he was sorry for anything or never admitted he was wrong (sound familiar?). Once a patient came to Doctor Kutchokokoff complaining about stomach pains.

"It is obvious," said Doctor Kutchokokoff, "your bowels are locked up!"

"Oh, no, doctor!" the patient exclaimed. "I have had the trots all day!"

"That is what I mean," said Doctor Kutchokokoff, with no apology. "Your bowels are locked wide open!"

Eventually, at the appointed time, Cornelius found himself sitting in the office of Doctor Kutchokokoff.

"My friend, and good doctor, Doctor Kutchokokoff, I find myself seeking your help, from both a personal and professional perspective (coughs uncomfortably and clears throat), as you see, I am an old white man, and unexpectedly -- and believe me -- I am having trouble articulating this -- well, there is a situation that I never expected to face, as you see, I now find myself with <u>too many children</u>."

Surprised, Doctor Kutchokokoff asked, "Cornelius! What did you just say?"

"I have **too many children**," Cornelius reiterated.

"You're going to have to tell me more about this!" Kutchokokoff exclaimed.

Pausing to compose himself, fidgeting a bit, Cornelius finally began. Not so long ago, driven by unexplained carnal impulses, I married a much younger woman. A mere six months after our first coitus she delivered a baby boy. That alone might have been tolerable, however she had unexpectedly brought three additional little ones from previous encounters, of which I had not known, but most likely, in hindsight, must have been among many adventures she has had in her young adventurous life.

"Great Mother-of-God," Kutchokokoff said. "You got yourself a flipping house full of little bastards!"

"Oh," Cornelius added, "her mother moved in, too, and I must say she is at times a most unpleasant person."

"At times?" asked Kutchokokoff.

"Well," Cornelius admitted, "...all of the time."

Cornelius stared blankly into space for a moment. "Anyway, Doc., I go <u>too many children</u>."

As I previously said, Doctor Kutchokokoff was a vain old white man who seldom was at a loss for words. This time, however, it took him a moment before he said, "This is a new one, even for me, so I must consult by medical book."

Kutchokokoff removed a large, black book from a shelf behind his desk. Thumbing through the book he kept repeating, "Too many children, too many children, too many children, too many children...." Finally he stopped on a page.

"Here it is," Kutchokokoff said. "Too many children, remove left testicle."

"What?" Cornelius asked.

"Remove left testicle," Kutchokokoff reaffirmed.

"Well, is that not a bit extreme?"

"You got too many children, friend. That left nut has got to go!"

Thus it was that surgery was scheduled and finally performed, removing Cornelius' left testicle.

Much to the surprise of Cornelius, a few months later Lolita again began to swell around the middle and again, in a few months more, delivered another baby boy. How could this have happened?

Again in the office of Doctor Kutchokokoff, Cornelius explained his dilemma "I got too many children, Doc. Now there is one more! What am I to do?"

Again, Doctor Kutchokokoff thumbed through his big black medical book. "Too many children, too many children, too many children.... Oh yes, here it is: 'remove left testicle' is what it says, and that should do the trick!"

"Doc," Cornelius replied, "we have already done that. You cut off my left nut."

"Oh, yes," Kutchokokoff replied. "I knew that; I was just testing you for dementia."

"Doc, with all due respect, even a demented old white man should know if one of his nuts is cut off!"

"And I agree, Cornelius," Kutchokokoff said as he continued to thumb through the big black medical book. "Oh, yes," he said, "here it is. It says '...if removing left testicle does not work, remove the right testicle.' Looks like it is back to surgery for you!"

Thus it was that Cornelius was returned to surgery to have his remaining testicle removed.

It did not work.

Months later Cornelius was again in the office of Doctor Kutchokokoff. "She's pregnant again?" the doctor asked.

"Big as a blimp and about to burst," Cornelius replied.

"Look in the book, look in the book," Kutchokokoff said. "Too many children, too many children, too many children. Oh yes, here it is: remove left testicle...."

"Done that, doctor," Cornelius said with dismay.

Again thumbing through to big black book, "...remove right testicle...."

"Done that."

Looking through the big black medical book, Doctor Kutchokokoff began to look surprised.

"Great Mother-of-God," Doctor Kutchokokoff cried. "I have cut the nuts off the wrong old white man!"

That's it.

That's the joke.

Silly Old White Man, Specimen 3

"Sad Sack"

[28]

REAL PEOPLE?

"SOBER TOMORROW"
(Apocryphal Story)

"Apocryphal" is an adjective, meaning something unverified and doubtful, although it is widely told as the truth (Like everything you hear on Fox News).

Sir Winston Churchill was drunk at a dinner party where he encountered Gertrude Stein and Alice B Toklas. Observing Sir Winston's inebriated condition, Gertrude remarked, "Sir Winston! You are drunk! ...disgustingly drunk!"

"Yes," replied Sir Winston, "but tomorrow morning I will be sober. But you, my dear Gertrude, you will still be ugly – disgustingly ugly!"

... I don't think this conversation ever really happened, but let us not let facts get in the way of a good story. Remember Mark Twain said, "The truth is a valuable thing; that is why I use it so sparingly."

COSTUMES

Pierpont and Cornelius loved to dress up
in costumes, as do most old white men.
They especially liked to dress up as
celebrity women, which is how we see them
attired here.

JUST BECOME A SAINT

Letter, Pierpont to Cornelius,

I am sorry to hear about your struggle with clinical depression. I understand that being an old white man can be depressing. Lolita took your money and left you, but at least she left the children – hers and yours (if, indeed, some of those were yours....) However, I have an idea: why not try being a saint instead? Mother Teresa has been dead for twenty years, right? I mean she is really dead. But some Catholics just voted that she is now a saint. Now, she's not quite dead anymore; she has to answer prayers from people wanting things that violate God's laws of physics, or, things that are highly improbable, like things that are a billion-to-one improbable. That is what saints do: they answer unreasonable requests from selfish people -- the assholes you do not like to be around but with whom you will spend eternity with in Heaven.

We have already determined that Heaven is not a place you want to go. Remember all those horrible people you knew that will be in Heaven? So, stay away from Heaven.

Consider being a saint. It should be a cushy job. Usually the answer to a prayer is, "No! Go fuck yourself!" That part is easy, right? Most of the bullshit requests saints receive provoke a negative response.

But this law of physics thing is interesting. To become a saint Mother Teresa had to have two "miracle" things to her credit; as I just said miracles are things that violate God's laws of physics. Supposedly one old woman got rid of some tumours after praying to Mother Teresa. Some old man had a similar "miracle." Funny thing, as I understand it, Mother Teresa was already dead when they prayed to her but she was not yet a saint. Explain that one to me.

Anyway, thought you might want to consider the becoming-a-saint thing. You don't have to be a Catholic; you could form your own church and then make a sainthood conversion committee to decide who would be saints. That way you could easily rig the system to get sainthood for yourself.

There are two things on the downside: (1) You must die (unless you change the rules). (2) You got to listen to prayers from a bunch of selfish assholes who want you to violate God's laws of physics for their benefit (but you could just get a prayer answering machine with a recorded messages that says, "No! Go fuck yourself!")

Best of luck and hope you find this helpful.

Cornelius replies:

All that sounds good and being a saint might be better than being an old white man. The deal breaker is that you have to die first; I'm glad that there may be a way around that.

Incidentally, I love Mother Teresa; she was, at least figuratively, a saint even before she died. So do not disparage the fine women.

As you know, I do not go to church. However, from time to time, I pray – but only to Mother Teresa.

Hope you all are well.

Pierpont,

I just read about a curious new weapon being developed by the U.S. At over 400 mph a fighter deploys a canister about the size of a bomb. But the canister slows and opens deploying hundreds of drones, about one pound each, on parachutes. After the drones lose their parachutes they assemble in formation. Why? I can't think of a single reason. But now you have hundreds, perhaps thousands, of one pound drones flying in enemy territory in a swarm.

This was a supposedly secret weapon which was leaked. Maybe leaking it was itself a plot to get enemies of the United States to spend money on similar weapons?

What do you make of it?

Hope all is well. It is like summertime here.

You could load each drone with two ounces of white bird guano and have them drop the sh#t on Kim Yong what's-his-name... ??

Silly Old White Man, Specimen 4

"The Evangelist"

[36]

BONUS SECTION!

POEMS BY WYCLIFFE HORSE

MY NAMESAKE SHIT

"Namesake" ... *a thing or person with the same name as another thing or person*

Buy that shit that has my name
I make money that way
I've never actually seen the shit
But make me some money; buy that shit.

Why oh why won't you buy that shit?
With my name on it it's probably OK
But really
I don't give a shit
Just buy that shit
My namesake shit.

I hear that shit is made by starving people
Who are maybe killed or maimed making
that shit.
Sad.
But hey
I don't give a shit
Just buy that shit
My namesake shit.
No shit
Buy that shit.

BETTER THAN GOING TO CHURCH

The commode overflowed
And it was right after I had filled
It with a generous portion
Of my ripe excrement
It wet my shoes
It wet my crumpled pants
That were neatly crumpled
Around my ankles
It stank
It was awful
But it was better than going to church!

I go golfing on Sundays
Willie died
My good friend Willie
Died on the Seventh Hole
So the rest of the game
It was hit the ball; drag Willie
Hit the ball; drag Willie
Eleven holes
Hit the ball; drag Willie
But it was better than going to church!

It finally happened
Israel bombed the Arabs
With the nuclear bombs
Given to them by the U.S.A.
The Arabs bombed back

With the nuclear bombs
We did not know they had
We are all dying
Of radiation poisoning
The Whole World is dying
But is better than going to church!

God or what's his name
Finally came
He, with a capital "H"
Decided none of us are worthy
Of Heaven
Now we are burning in a Lake of Fire,
Forever
We are forced to eat our own excrement
But guess what?
It is better than going to church!

PREACHER BOB

An old white man

Tenor voice:
I am going down to the big old church
The one with a lot of glass
Going to give Bob my money
I am going to kiss his ass!

Baritone voice:
"Asp," it is a snake
Snake handling
Praise the Lord

Tenor voice:
I gave Bob my money
And my thirteen-year-old-daughter
Is pregnant
I think Bob may be the dad.

Baritone voice:
Lo it is the child of Jesus
Your daughter is pure.

Tenor voice:
Bob says my donated money
Will come back to me ten times
Sorry about your daughter,

Bob – I mean Jesus --
Was just having him a good time

Baritone voice:
Snake handling
You probably do not appreciate
That pun ….

Tenor voice:
The church secretary was Betty
She got pregnant; I don't understand
Her husband died a long time ago
In a place called Afghanistan
Now Betty is missing
And so is the church treasury
Bob proposes she took the cash
And decided to flee.

Baritone voice:
They will never find the body.

Falsetto voice:
Look in the church dumpster.

Tenor voice:
Bob got a brand new Bentley
Which is a very expensive automobile.

Baritone voice:
My church is not like your church
I am better than you

God has chosen me
And all your stuff is mine.

Tenor voice:
You are going to hell
But I will be OK
God loves me
Not you

Falsetto voice:
Look in the church dumpster.

Tenor voice:
I'm going down to the big old church
The one with a lot of glass
I'm going down to the big old church
I'm a going to kiss Bob's ass.

Banjo Solo Here

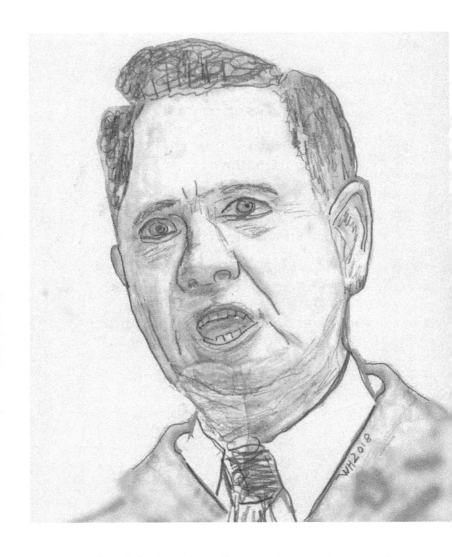

Silly Old White Man, Specimen 5
"The Judge"

BABY GOT THE GUN

Baby got the gun and he done shot mama
Plugged that bitch right through the heart
Papa left the handgun on the floor by Baby
Plugged that bitch right through the heart!

Baby got the gun and he done shot brother
Shot brother's right arm plum clear off
Papa left the shotgun on the floor by Baby
Shot brother's right arm plum clear off!

Baby got the gun and he done shot sister
Plugged that bitch right in the eye
Papa left the pistol on the floor by Baby
Plugged that bitch right in the eye!

Baby got the gun and he done shot Papa
Little bastard won't be shooting no more
That silly old white man Papa
Is dead with his guns on the goddamned floor!

STICK IT IN CRAZY

Don't stick your thing in Crazy.

That is certainly what I went and done

I stuck it in Crazy

Damn, it was fun!

Yeah, she was good on the trapeze.

She wore jewellery in unexpected places.

Most of her tattoos were spelled correctly.

And I sure as hell did not know that you could do that with that....

It was crazy, crazy fun for a while,

Even after I caught the rash.

And my crotch looked like hash.

Why did you not tell me that this activity would make babies?

The goddamned critters are crawling out of the flipping woodwork.

Little bastards are everywhere.

Is it because I stuck it in Crazy?

Well, what is a guy supposed to do? God made me this way.

I stuck my dick in Crazy.

That is all I will say.

Except that I need some more of that medical cream that temporarily stops it from itching.

Isn't that bitching?

HOLLYWOOD VACATION

I went to Hollywood to have some fun
But the celebrities there kept chasing me bum
Trying to touch me bum
That wasn't fun
At least not for me.

An actor who seemed a wee bit spacey
Touched my private placey
He didn't even kiss me first.

Then there was the rubber faced funny man
I think he dropped some pills in my soda can

I can't say for sure but a few hours later
I woke up stunned
With a very sore and bleeding bum.

A producer named Harvey
With the morals of black fly larvae
Whipped out his tally whacker and yelled,
"You want some of this?"
"You want some of this?"
I did not have the appetite for such a thing
And besides, his thing smelled bad,
Like stinky cheese.

Then an old male actor suggested felching,

Said it would taste better with
Roquefort dressing.
I don't think so.

Next time I will be taking my vacation
In Dolomite Alabama.
Where my anatomical structures will
be safer.
And nobody there knows what a rim
job is.

~~~~

REALITY STARS

They have no talent but they got riches
Taking off bras and under britches
They can't sing and they can't dance
But there they are
Without underpants.

They make sex videos as very young debs,
And somehow leak them on the World Wide Web

Their sex lives are public, the real and the fiction
The girls get knocked up
What rhymes with "fiction"?
Friction?
Yes, there is a lot of that.
Pass the butter.

Silly Old White Man, Specimen 6

"The Aristocrat"

EVEN MORE OLD WHITE MEN JOKES

The Empire State Building

Why did the old white man jump off the Empire State Building?

He wanted to be a smash on Broadway!

Why did the old white man throw the butter off the Empire State Building?

Because he wanted to see a butterfly!

Why did the old white man throw margarine off the Empire State Building?

He wanted to see an imitation butterfly.

Why did the old white man throw his wrist watch off the Empire State Building?

He wanted to see time fly.

Why did the old white man drive his truck off the Empire State Building?

He wanted to test his air brakes.

So, how did the old white man get his truck on top of the Empire State Building?

He jumped it across from the Chrysler Building.

...and then....

What did the old white man do when he learned that he was going to die?

He went into the living room.

Why did the very little old white man drown in the kitchen sink?

He was trying to learn tap dancing.

Why did the old white man drive his car into a tree?

He wanted to hear its bark.

Teacher: "Have you ever read Shakespeare?"

Old white man: "No, who wrote it?"

An old white man is buying a TV. "Do you have colour TVs?"

"Sure."

"Give me a green one, please."

A old white man calls airport. "How long does it take to fly to London?"

"Just a sec," says the rep.

"Thank you." says the old white man and hangs up.

An old white man was filling up an application form for a job. He promptly filled the columns titled name, age, address, etc.

Then he came to the column "Salary Expected":

He was not sure as to what to be filled there.

After much thought he wrote:

"Yes."

Silly Old White Man, Specimen 7

"The Economist"

You Can Recognize An Old White Man By Observing If He ....

- Puts lipstick on the forehead because he wants to make up his mind.
- Gets stabbed in a shoot-out.
- Sends a fax with a postage stamp on it.
- Tries to drown a fish in waters.
- Thinks socialism means partying.
- Trips over a cordless phone.
- Takes a ruler to bed to see how long he slept.
- At the bottom of the application where it says "Sign Here" he puts "Sagittarius."

- Studies for a blood test and fails.
- Sells the car for gas money.
- Misses the 44 bus, and takes the 22 twice instead.
- Drives to the airport and sees a sign that said, "Airport left", he turns around and goes home.
- Gets locked in a furniture shop and sleeps on the floor.

ALLIGATOR BOOTS

An old white man proposes to a woman.

She says, yes if you bring me a pair of alligator boots.

He sets off to Florida and disappears. Finally a search is made.

They find him hunting alligators and watch him killing a huge one.

He walks over to the reptile, checks its legs and angrily exclaims, "I have now killed over one hundred of these things, and this one, like all the others, is barefoot!"

THE THERMOS BOTTLE

An old white man goes into a store and, sees a shiny object.

He asks the clerk, "What is that shiny object?"

The clerk replies, "That is a thermos bottle."

The old white man then asks, "What does it do?"

The clerk responds, "It keeps hot things hot and it keeps cold things cold."

The old white man says, "I'll take it!"

The next day, he walks into work with his new thermos.

His old white man boss sees him and asks, "What is that shiny object with you?"

He said, "It's a thermos bottle."

The boss then says, "What does it do?"

He replies, "It keeps hot things hot and cold things cold."

The boss said, "Wow, what do you have in it?"

The old white man replies, "Two cups of hot coffee and a glass of iced tea."

A variation of this joke goes:

The clerk says, "This thermos bottle keeps hot liquids hot, and it keeps cold liquids cold."

Confused, the old white man asks, "How does it know?"

MAKING COPIES

What will an old white man do if he wants an additional white sheet of paper?

(He already has one and he wants one more.)

He takes a photocopy of the white paper!!!

What will an old white man do after taking photocopies?

He will compare it with the original for spelling mistakes!

THE PHONE CALL

It was three o'clock in the morning when the old white man's phone rang, so he trudged from his seventh-floor bedroom all the way down to the ground-floor drawing-room to answer it.

"Hello?" said the old white man.

"Hello" said the voice at the other end. "Is that one-one-one-one-one-one?"

"No", said the old white man. "This is eleven-eleven-eleven."

"Oh," said the voice at the other end, "I must have the wrong number. I'm terribly sorry for disturbing you."

"Oh, that's all right", said the old white man. "I had to get up anyway to answer this blasted phone!"

ARE WE BEATING A DEAD HORSE?

Although limited in word count, you no longer worry about getting your money's worth from this book. You just want it to be over.

OK, it's over.

~~~~~~

BIBLIOGRAPHY

Forty Yards to the Outhouse, by Willie Make-It

The Yellow River, by I.P. Freely

The Ruptured Man, by One Hung Low

Under the Stadium, by Seymour Butts

Tiger Attack, by Claude Ballz

Rustle in the Bushes, by Willie Get-It

Antlers in the Treetops, by Who-Goosed-the-Moose

~~~~~~

THE AUTHOR

Wycliffe Horse

Born in a tiny tar paper shack in Dolomite, Alabama, Wycliffe Horse is now a literary giant. Known best for his timeless writing, Wycliffe can also eat a whole lot of raw oysters. He likes crab meat, too.

~~~~~~

CPSIA information can be obtained
at www.ICGtesting.com
Printed in the USA
LVHW040926221219
641386LV00004B/1442